5 Skills for the Global Learner

T0349510

CORWIN CONNECTED EDUCATORS SERIES

Blogging for Educators: Writing for Professional Learning
By Starr Sackstein @mssackstein

Principal Professional Development: Leading Learning in the Digital Age
By Joseph Sanfelippo @Joesanfelippofc and Tony Sinanis @TonySinanis

The Power of Branding: Telling Your School's Story
By Tony Sinanis @TonySinanis and Joseph Sanfelippo @Joesanfelippofc

The Relevant Educator: How Connectedness Empowers Learning
By Tom Whitby @tomwhitby and Steven W. Anderson @web20classroom

In memory of Fredda Barnes, who believed in me first.

You are in my thoughts, and you are missed.

5 Skills for the Global Learner

What Everyone Needs to
Navigate the Digital World

Mark Barnes

A SAGE Company

CORWIN
A SAGE Company

FOR INFORMATION:

Corwin

A SAGE Company

2455 Teller Road

Thousand Oaks, California 91320

(800) 233-9936

www.corwin.com

SAGE Publications Ltd.

1 Oliver's Yard

55 City Road

London EC1Y 1SP

United Kingdom

SAGE Publications India Pvt. Ltd.

B 1/I 1 Mohan Cooperative Industrial Area

Mathura Road, New Delhi 110 044

India

SAGE Publications Asia-Pacific Pte. Ltd.

3 Church Street

#10-04 Samsung Hub

Singapore 049483

Printed in the United States of America

A catalog record of this book is available from the Library of Congress.

ISBN 978-1-4833-8291-3

This book is printed on acid-free paper.

Executive Editor: Arnis Burvikovs

Associate Editor: Ariel Price

Editorial Assistant: Andrew Olson

Production Editor: Amy Schroller

Copy Editor: Kimberly Hill

Typesetter: C&M Digitals (P) Ltd.

Proofreader: Penelope Sippel

Cover and Interior Designer: Janet Kiesel

Marketing Manager: Lisa Lysne

Certified Chain of Custody
Promoting Sustainable Forestry
www.sfiprogram.org
SFI-01268

SFI label applies to text stock

15 16 17 18 19 10 9 8 7 6 5 4 3 2 1

Contents

Preface

Welcome to the Corwin Connected Educators Series.

Last year, Ariel Price, Arnis Burvikovs, and I assembled a great list of authors for the fall 2014 books in the Corwin Connected Educators Series. As leaders in their field of connected education, they all provided practical, short books that helped educators around the world find new ways to connect. The books in the spring 2015 season will be equally as beneficial for educators.

We have all seen momentous changes for educators. States debate the use of the Common Core State Standards, and teachers and leaders still question the use of technology, while some of their students have to disconnect and leave it at home because educators do not know how to control learning on devices. Many of the Series authors worked in schools where they were sometimes the only ones trying to encourage use of technology tools at the same time their colleagues tried to ban it. Through their PLNs they were able to find others who were trying to push the envelope.

This spring, we have a list of authors who are known for pushing the envelope. Some are people who wrote books for the fall 2014 season, while others are new to the series. What they have in common is that they see a different type of school for students, and they write about ideas that all schools should be practicing now.

Rafranz Davis discusses *The Missing Voices in EdTech*. She looks at and discusses how we need to bring more diverse voices to the connected world because those voices will enrich how we learn and the way we think. Starr Sackstein, a teacher in New York City writes about blogging for reflection in her book *Blogging for Educators*. Twitter powerhouse Steven W. Anderson returns to the Series to bring us *Content Curation,* as do the very engaging Joseph M. Sanfelippo and Tony Sinanis with their new book, *Principal Professional Development*. Mark Barnes rounds out the comeback authors with his book on *5 Skills for the Global Learner*. Thomas C. Murray and Jeffrey Zoul bring a very practical "how-to" for teachers and leaders in their book *Leading Professional Learning,* and Makerspaces extraordinaire Laura Fleming brings her expertise with *Worlds of Making*.

I am insanely excited about this book series. As a former principal, I know time is in short supply, and teachers and leaders need something they can read today and put into practice tomorrow. That is the exciting piece about technology; it can help enhance your practices by providing you with new ideas and helping you connect with educators around the world.

The books can be read in any order, and each will provide information on the tools that will keep us current in the digital age. We also look forward to continuing the series with more books from experts on connectedness.

As Michael Fullan has been saying for many years, technology is not the right driver, good pedagogy is, and the books in this connected series focus on practices that will lead to good pedagogy in our digital age. To assist readers in their connected experience, we have created the Corwin Connected Educators companion website where readers can connect with the authors and find resources to help further their experience. The website can be found at www.corwin.com/connectededucators. It is our hope that we can meet you where you are in your digital journey and bring you up to the next level.

Peter M. DeWitt, EdD
@PeterMDeWitt

Acknowledgments

Not so long ago, I thought Twitter and Facebook were just trendy places to share family pictures and tell people what kind of latte you're drinking. Then, I learned that these and other social networks are vibrant online neighborhoods, bustling with some of the world's most intelligent teachers. My Personal Learning Network has become a vast library of knowledge and my most valuable resource. When I have questions, I ask my PLN for help. The answers come instantly and from all over the world. Now, this is power. For everyone in this wonderful online neighborhood, thanks for helping me make this book a lot smarter than it would be without you. Thanks to Ariel Price, Arnis Burvikovs, and Peter DeWitt for inviting me to be part of the Corwin Connected Educators Series. I believe these books are improving education and I'm proud to be part of this remarkable team. Thanks Andrew Olson for doing a lot of the behind-the-scenes work that is thankless but necessary. Thank you Kimberly Hill for your sharp eye. Thanks Starr Sackstein for being my go-to person, when I need examples of amazing education technology in action. Thanks to the people who responded to my requests for the anecdotes shared in this book. You know who you are, and I appreciate your time and your dedication to our profession. A special thanks to my parents, brothers, and sisters for their unwavering patience. You continue to invite me to picnics, no matter how many times I say, "I can't make it; I'm writing." Thanks Ethan and Lauren for bringing joy to my life. Special thanks to my wife Mollie. You prop me up when I'm falling down.

About the Author

 **Mark Barnes** is a veteran classroom teacher, keynote speaker, and author of many education books, including the critically acclaimed *Role Reversal: Achieving Uncommonly Excellent Results in the Student-Centered Classroom* (ASCD, 2013), *The 5-Minute Teacher* (ASCD, 2013), and *Assessment 3.0: Throw Out Your Grade Book and Inspire Learning* (Corwin, 2015). Mark's *Teaching the iStudent* (2014) is part of the initial launch of Corwin's Connected Educators Series. A longtime adjunct professor at two Ohio colleges, Mark has created five online courses on web-based instruction, mobile learning, and using Twitter in the classroom and as a professional development tool. A leading expert on student-centered learning, Mark has helped thousands of educators build digitally enhanced, project-based, no-grades classrooms. Mark is the creator of the internationally recognized how-to video site for educators, Learn it in 5, and publisher of the popular *Brilliant or Insane*, named a Top 10 education technology blog by *EdTech Magazine* in 2014. Mark's TED talk, *How Four Simple Words Can Solve Education's Biggest Problem,* is a tribute to the worldwide movement toward alternative assessment practices. His Facebook group, Teachers Throwing Out Grades, along with his Assessment 3.0 Facebook page represent a growing collection of global educators dedicated to eliminating traditional grades and using technology and social media to provide meaningful feedback to students. A highly regarded connected educator, Mark can be found on Twitter at @markbarnes19.

Introduction

The students read a book. They read in the United States and Canada, while others read in Australia and in Korea. They discussed the story, and they wrote about it. What's the big deal, you may wonder; it's certainly not unusual for students to read in school. Perhaps not, but what makes these students unique is that they read and discussed the same book at the same time collaboratively, from classrooms scattered across thousands of miles of land and sea, as part of the Global Read Aloud Project. Not so long ago, the distance between these children would have been an impenetrable barrier. In today's digital world, however, distance and cultural differences are inconsequential. In the right environment, with appropriate tools, under the tutelage of properly trained guides, the 21st-century global learner can connect with billions of teachers anytime from any classroom from all corners of the world. And projects like the Global Read Aloud provide the backdrop for revolutionary acquisition and sharing of knowledge and skills. Most important, projects such as this spark a virtual dialogue that unites learners. Global Read Aloud creator Pernille Ripp describes the power of the project this way:

> The sheer act of reading is intimate; yet when you use the power of a read aloud to connect students globally, we recreate that cocoon of safety all across the world. When we let the strangers in, when we allow others through our armor, we let the moment create a way to

start a discussion. So reading aloud the same book to students around the world ignites a global conversation. One that starts in a safe place for all these children, one that can lead to deeper connections, more empathy, and definitely more sharing of a love of books. (2014)

THE GLOBAL LEARNER

Students in elementary schools, middle and high schools, and many in colleges participate in the Global Read Aloud Project each year. These children, young adults and educators are perfect models of the global learner—someone who collaborates with other teachers and learners across all borders and barriers, using 21st-century digital tools to start and join powerful conversations about learning. The global learner is not a student in the strictest interpretation of the word (we tend to think of students as children, teenagers, and young adults in their twenties who may be pursuing advanced degrees). Global learning is not restricted by age or experience. The ubiquity of mobile devices has placed the Internet in the palm of our hands. This also puts literally billions of teachers and resources a finger swipe or voice command away.

So, global learners are pre–K–12 students. They are college students, but they are also schoolteachers and professors; they are firefighters, bankers, and landscapers. The global learner is a lifelong learner, who uses every available resource to create, maintain, and share content in a classroom or work place and with people around the world. The global learner is a content curator, who understands that with every word she reads and writes and with each picture or video she tweets or likes, she is both a teacher and a student. When we read a book or draw a picture, we grow; we learn. The second we interact with content and share it in person or online, we become global students and, in essence, global teachers. In the digital world, these two people are the same. The remainder of this book will examine and illustrate this concept.

LEAVING A DIGITAL FOOTPRINT

Whether you realize it or not, you most likely have a digital footprint. Skeptical? Grab the closest mobile device, open Google, type your name in the search box and locate your footprint. Even if just a handful of tweets represent the bedrock of your social media activity, you will find yourself some place in that Google search. Once you become part of any digital record—a local news story, a blog post, part of a public report, such as school board minutes or, gasp, the police blotter—you exist online and you leave a digital footprint. People who are relatively inactive Internet users leave a passive footprint, but as social networks and mobile devices expand, active footprints are becoming commonplace. With the evolution of technology, students and teachers will undoubtedly create active digital footprints—indentations made online by the web pages, blogs, social media activity and emails they post. As social learning and content curation grow, students' digital footprints will also expand.

Understanding its meaning and the importance of this footprint is essential for global learners. College admissions deans and job recruiters will scrutinize what students are curating and how they are using the abundant information that the Internet provides. Your digital footprint tells a story about you. This is one more piece of a growing responsibility for teachers to educate students about the impact that social media and the digital world have on both their present and their future lives. "We want to ensure that our voices are the ones telling our story—we cannot let anyone else tell our story for us" (Sinanis & Sanfelippo, 2014, p. 7). The five global learning skills outlined in this book all contribute to one's digital footprint. As you learn these skills and consider how you might teach them to others, also consider how they impact the creation of a digital footprint.

MOBILE DEVICES

It can be argued that at one time pencil and paper were a student's most useful tools. However, it's difficult to deny that the mobile device powers most activity in the daily life of the global learner. Understanding the impact that smartphones, tablets, eReaders, and other mobile devices have on learning is critical to not only all of today's students but also to all educators. "It is plausible that before this decade ends, all students, even many in elementary schools, will have a smartphone or a similar Internet-ready device" (Barnes, 2014, p. 22). Knowing that they are working with global learners, teachers must do all they can to harness the magnificent power of mobile devices for learning. There will be more on how this is done throughout the book, because as mobile tools evolve, how these devices influence global learning evolves, too.

 CONNECTED MOMENT

The effective global learner is always considering the power of technology to reach a worldwide audience. When global learners create or share content, they are always mindful of how it molds their digital footprint. They are keenly aware of how the content crosses digital divides.

AN OCEAN OF RESOURCES

Global learners understand that Apple and Google offer millions of applications—most of which can be used for learning. In fact, both technology giants offer a massive suite of education tools, and software magnate Microsoft is joining this growing industry. In its infant stage of development, this book's working title was *5 Tools for the Global Learner*. My goal was to identify the five most important digital learning and content curation tools that intelligent teachers and students use. Thankfully, I realized just how dubious this notion was. The Internet contains an ocean of resources. Ask any connected educator to name the most important ones and, while there are sure to be some similar answers, their responses would likely compose a litany of important web tools. Some of these will be shared in later chapters. The idea that there is one go-to list of tools for global learners is unrealistic. Mainly because the tools that students and teachers choose are a matter of preference (you may like Pinterest for website curation, while I may prefer Feedly). Plus, the constant evolution of the Internet brings with it an ephemeral quality; in other words, as new websites, software, and social networks crop up, they make many of their predecessors obsolete. Twitter would most certainly have made my top 5 list, and while I believe Twitter is here to stay, it's not unreasonable to believe that it may one day be replaced by something that doesn't currently exist. This is why digital skills are far more important than tools. The best global learners can adapt their skills to any device, website, or application, as long as global learners have attained the skills that are necessary to navigate the digital divide.

5 CRUCIAL SKILLS

As naming the five most important web tools or apps may be impossible, singling out the skills necessary for effective global learning is also challenging. Let me be completely transparent here. While I am widely regarded as an expert in education technology, mobile learning, and social media, I don't believe that any one person has the experience to say that a particular list of skills is the only worthwhile list of skills for global learning. This list was composed after much contemplation and discussion with friends, colleagues, and luminary connected educators. My hope is that this list will serve as a discussion starter. Perhaps in time, all of us will collaborate on an updated list of skills. In the meantime, here are five skills that I believe every global learner should have:

1. Creating and Sharing Digital Information

2. Using Social Media for Worldwide Sharing

3. Digital Publishing

4. Building a Personal Learning Network

5. Using Aggregators to Create, Maintain, and Share Content

Subsequent chapters will examine each of these skills and provide anecdotes and examples of various web tools that someone might use to demonstrate what everyone needs to navigate the digital world.

● ● ● ● REFLECTION

Have you considered your own digital footprint? What would a student or your own child find if he or she Googled you? How does your digital footprint define you? Do you embrace mobile learning and web tools in your classroom or at your school? Consider the impact of mobile devices, applications, and each of the 5 global learning skills introduced here. Are you maximizing these tools and skills, so you can become a global learner and a global teacher? Are there critical skills that are not mentioned here? The discussion continues on Twitter at hashtag #CorwinCE. Add your thoughts there as you read this book, and when you finish it.

CHAPTER 1

Creating and Sharing Digital Information

Today's students are speaking out to their teachers loudly and clearly: They want activities and assignments in school that allow them to create content and share it with others.

—Jared Covili, author
Going Google: Powerful Tools for 21st-Century Learning

I n 2008, I was presenting classroom websites at an education technology conference in Columbus, called eTech Ohio. Before my session, Chris Carman, a teacher from Kent, Ohio, delivered a presentation on screencasting—something I'd never heard of before that day. I can't recall a time when I was so completely mesmerized by a presentation. During a time when I was becoming somewhat advanced in technology integration, I knew nothing about what is arguably the most important skill teachers and students can have. As Carman expertly explained how to capture a computer screen, or upload a slide show, and narrate it, using a screencasting application, my mind raced, crafting one possibility after another for my classroom. I wanted digital instruction but until then I wasn't sure how to deliver it. On a wintry February day at a convention center in Columbus, Chris Carman helped me become a global educator, and neither one of us knew it.

> The almost ineffable, yet beautiful, quality of the screencast is its ability to remove the teacher from the front of the classroom.

If you are still confused by screencasting, consider the Khan Academy. Salman Khan, a hedge fund manager turned video producer, began creating instructional videos in 2003 so he could help his cousin with math. Khan produced problems on his computer and recorded them with a screen capture application. Then he narrated the lessons much like a teacher would do in class, while drawing something on a blackboard with chalk. History says Khan's friends and family liked the tutorials and wanted more, so the video educator decided to publish his screencasts to the world's largest online video library, YouTube. Eventually, the Khan Academy, which now houses thousands of videos with millions of viewers and has an educator-specific application, was born. Whether he did so intentionally or inadvertently, Sal Khan inspired people such as Chris Carman and contributed greatly to a new form of instruction—screencasting.

But what, precisely, makes screencasting a global learning skill? While this book is not designed as an endorsement for the Khan Academy, it's difficult to deny that Khan sparked a teaching and learning revolution with his online video tutorials. The Khan Academy is a venue for global learning, and whether one likes the Academy's videos or not, they exemplify a method of instruction that mobilizes lessons. When coupled with other digital tools, screencasts can create a global conversation about virtually any topic.

SCREENCASTING FOR TEACHING AND LEARNING

Although it's no longer in its infancy, screencasting is still a largely unknown, or at least misunderstood, education commodity. Today, most people know screencasts as videos—an imprecise, albeit practical, designation for an online tutorial created by recording a computer screen or slide show and, in most cases, narrating the recording. In effect, screencasts are interactive lessons. The almost ineffable, yet beautiful, quality of the screencast is its ability to remove the teacher from the front of the classroom. "Not only can screencasts be used to ignite remarkable five-minute instruction they can also become part of a growing web-based archive of brief videos that students can access at any time" (Barnes, 2013, p. 18).

JING

I made my first screencast video the day after seeing Chris Carman's presentation in 2008, using a free software tool. Jing Software, from TechSmith, a company that creates numerous screencasting and video editing tools, allows users to create up to five-minute videos, which is the perfect length for interactive teaching and learning. For years, I spent countless hours in my home office, recording slides, websites, videos, designs, and anything I believed might enhance classroom instruction. Eventually, I posted the videos on my classroom website, which comprised an ever-growing library of educational videos for students, parents, and other educators to see. It took a few more years for me to realize the power of screencasting as a global learning tool. Unlike other web-based video production services, Jing is downloadable software, which must be housed on a computer's hard drive. The simplicity of Jing makes it an excellent choice for teachers and students who have little or no experience with screen capture video creation. Other tools described in this chapter offer either web or mobile app versions, and some include both.

ANIMOTO AND OTHER SCREENCASTING TOOLS

I was teaching the literary term flashback to seventh graders in 2010. During my transition away from traditional teaching to a student-centered classroom, I produced one screencast after another, improving my technique each time. The length of the videos was always five minutes or less, and I added as many graphics and annotations as possible to engage young, often distracted, learners. To capture the essence of flashback as a device for understanding fiction, I found a brief video of a movie character remembering an event from earlier in his life. I recorded this movie moment using Jing and I narrated the video explaining key points of flashback, as the movie clip played. I could discuss the power of this instruction ad nauseam, but I prefer to share an anecdote from class, when I showed the flashback video. Students watched the expertly crafted video in silence, and I assumed they would all be able to teach the literary element when the screencast ended. The second the video stopped, an eager student's hand shot up. "How did you make that video?" the inquisitive 12-year-old asked. "Do you think I could do something like that for my project?" Only somewhat aggravated that the question wasn't about flashback, I explained how I created the video using a screencasting tool called Jing. "What's screencasting?" another student wondered out loud. Although few students were thinking about flashback at that time, what educators call a teachable moment occurred. Going to our classroom website's library of instructional presentations, which contained plenty of YouTube and TeacherTube videos,

I clicked into several screencasts I had fashioned and explained how they were fabricated. Suddenly, the room was buzzing with dozens of preteens all eager to begin producing videos that they could use later to demonstrate learning.

Because Jing is a software application that couldn't be downloaded to all school computers, we searched for alternative, web-based screencasting applications. Students discovered Animoto as a powerful substitute for Jing. Animoto is not screencasting, based on the narrowest definition, but it is video production. Although it's not a screen capture tool, Animoto is a website and mobile application that allows users to upload pictures, videos, music, and text. My students, most of whom embrace digital tools, were eager to integrate Animoto into projects in their English language arts class and in other subjects. They became especially excited when they realized that they could share their Animoto videos with not only their classmates, family and friends but also with the world. These energetic, creative learners started producing videos weekly (some daily), posting

> The ability to communicate with a global audience is the Internet's greatest gift to learners.

them to their blogs or class websites and sharing them with the world through social media. When a student reported friends from other states commenting on his Animoto video, this sparked interest from his friends, who also wanted to engage audiences outside of our classroom.

It struck me that my students were becoming global teachers and global learners. Peers outside of our classroom, school, and our city and state were communicating with my students providing feedback about their videos. The most amazing part of this serendipitous discovery was how students were demonstrating mastery learning while teaching others through screencasting. They embraced activities excitedly, never pausing to wonder if learning was boring, because it wasn't. Soon, Animoto wasn't enough to satisfy their appetites for digital teaching and learning. Almost weekly, someone announced a new tool, discovered over the weekend, which could be used for some sort of screencasting or video production. Some used Slide Rocket, a web-based presentation site similar to PowerPoint, with an array of modules that students loved. Other students liked ShowMe, which is a tablet application and allows users to interact directly with the app by drawing on the tablet and narrating the design. Of course, as is the case with most screencasting and video creation tools, the biggest benefit is the ability to share a personal media presentation to social networks, making each video or screencast interactive, which makes the producer a global teacher and learner.

 CONNECTED MOMENT

Flipped learning, which means using video outside of school to acquire new skills and concepts, became popular years ago. Screencasting makes digital instruction easy for both teachers and students. The student who can create a screencast about a particular concept or skill and share it with the world is on the path to becoming both a global learner and a global teacher—something all educators should want for their students.

DIGITAL COMMUNICATION

Recall how students broke the boundaries of the brick and mortar classroom during the Global Read Aloud. Essential to the success of global learning is that all shareholders have a common goal. The Global Read Aloud Project provides students with such a goal—read the same book and share its lessons. The ability to communicate with a global audience is the Internet's greatest gift to learners. Unfortunately, most students struggle to comprehend the value of the Internet and of social media as platforms for locating the billions of teachers that are literally now just a mouse click away. Children and teenagers often fail to find the common ground that will engage other teachers and learners outside of their classroom. This is where teachers play a critical role in global learning. We must illuminate the path to global communication. Teachers can guide students to incredible learning opportunities by shaping the goal and by igniting online conversation. There are many tools other than Facebook, Twitter, and Instagram—all worthy platforms—for creating a broad discussion

© Jupiter Images/Thinkstock Photos

about a common goal. The next section examines some specific applications and illustrates the power of cloud computing as a means of creating or strengthening ongoing global communication.

SKYPE, GOOGLE HANGOUTS, CLOUD COMPUTING

Fifth graders in a California school scramble around the classroom searching for maps on desktop computers and in textbooks. Meanwhile, their peers chat with students at another school in a faraway place via Skype's live online camera connection. As videographers from Microsoft capture their work, these remarkable digital learners collaborate with students in Mexico, showing the world that they too believe in teaching and learning across barriers (*Mystery Skype*, 2014). They ask each other about landscape, weather trends, and potential surrounding cities. The teachers circulate and observe, playing only a small role in the student-centered classrooms. "Are you in Mexico City?" one inquirer asks a peer on a computer screen. She answers yes, and the classroom erupts in cheers, as the mystery has been solved.

Skype is one of many online tools that can instantaneously beam teachers and learners into classrooms all around the world. Skype and Hangouts, Google's answer to the online face-to-face conversation, facilitate global communication. These and other cloud-based applications build an ongoing discussion about learning and help students realize that billions of teachers are just a mouse click or a tablet swipe away. Skype and Google Hangouts encourage even the shiest students to engage in activities, because these video tools bring strangers into the safe confines of the students' familiar environment. While it might take many American 10-year-olds weeks or months to talk to a Mexican enrollee, all will interact with students whose faces are merely 3D images emitted on a computer screen. These online discussion tools that bring people who are thousands of miles apart together in a virtual classroom help students develop communication skills that are crucial to teaching and learning in the digital world.

● ● ● ● REFLECTION

In what ways do your students share learning with you, with their peers, and with others outside the walls of your classroom? Consider teaching students how to create a screencast that demonstrates learning and produces a video that can be shared both in and out of the classroom. Plan a meeting with a class in another country, using Skype or Google Hangouts. Discuss the value of screencasting and video conferencing as global teaching and learning skills. Ask your students how these skills can serve them in the future.

CHAPTER
2

Using Social Media for Worldwide Sharing

From the beginning of time, humans have communicated in some way, shape, or form. Whether the method was writing on cave walls or is today's tweeting, people have and always will leverage the power of available technology to stay connected.

—Brad Currie, author
All Hands on Deck: Tools for Connecting Educators,
Parents, and Communities

The voices in the faculty lounge thundered around the room, and I quickly shut the door behind me, so students in adjacent classes would not hear their teachers shouting. When I turned the corner, I realized it was just one teacher, and she wasn't yelling at her colleagues in argument; rather, she was venting about an incident in her classroom, and her voice had elevated to a quavering crescendo. What could be so upsetting after just three class periods? I wondered aloud. The teacher replayed her story, to the chagrin of others who had tolerated it once already, explaining that she had caught a student surreptitiously posting to Facebook during class. "I'm so sick of the phones and the social networks," the storyteller complained. "They do nothing but disrupt my class." I acknowledged her with a nod, as I retrieved my lunch from the refrigerator 10 feet from the table where the five educators were huddled. Perched on my toes so I could gather in a plate at the top of a cabinet, I asked the teacher, "What if you encouraged all your students to use their electronic devices and invited them to share what they know on a social network that you create?" The frustrated teacher shook her head, harrumphed, and quickly exited the room. Just before she reached the door she said, "That will be the day." Sadly, the dawn of mobile device use and social networking was just beginning for some teachers at my school, while most remained rooted in traditional practices, which called for a ban of electronic devices in the classroom.

"Even though one-to-one schools (one computer per student), cloud computing, and mobile learning are becoming popular around the world, many school districts and their employees have only scratched the surface of understanding the power and importance of digital learning" (Barnes, 2014, p. 3). If we are to inspire global learning, though, the leave-mobile-devices-at-home attitudes must stop. Global learners have incredible power at their fingertips, and educators must embrace this power. This means investing in students as curators of information and helping them create, maintain, and share content worldwide. "With social media, we are creating our own personal newspapers that can be read by others and even picked up in the mainstream press. With that in mind, it is an easier reminder that, whenever you write, ask yourself how you would feel if what you wrote were in tomorrow's newspaper" (Nielsen, 2014). Social media is the best vehicle for global sharing. Our students have been using it for many years, and if we encourage social networking for learning, not just the sky but cyberspace is the limit.

TWITTER

Recall the introduction, when I admitted that this book could have been a Best Tools list. If it were a list of the most powerful tools for global learning, Twitter certainly would have made the cut. With real-time hashtag discussions, like #EdChat, #EdTechChat, and #Principalpln, connecting educators around the world daily, Twitter has become the go-to digital learning tool for teachers. In recent years, students have gravitated to Twitter, many abandoning social media kingpin, Facebook. "Teen Twitter use has grown significantly: 24% of online teens use Twitter, up from 16% in 2011" (Madden et al., 2013). Students may love the simplicity of Twitter's 140 characters, but once they begin using it in the classroom, students quickly realize that Twitter is much more than a "join-me-at-Starbucks" messaging service.

 CONNECTED MOMENT

If most students are using social media daily, it's important to help them understand the potential for learning on social networks, because many young learners see digital media as nothing more than a virtual playground—a place to share private pictures and personal stories. The best way to demonstrate the power of social networking for educational purposes is by using social media in the classroom, as a teaching and learning tool and, more important, as a means for building communication skills both in and out of the classroom.

Twitter is gaining traction as a conversation tool in classrooms, but the concept of using a social network to engage learners is not new. Years ago, a high school teacher in Los Angeles discovered Twitter at the Macworld Convention and experienced what he told CNN was "an aha moment." Enrique Legaspi taught his eighth graders how to use Twitter as a conversation tool, even though research back then contended that social media could interfere with learning. According to CNN (Simon, 2011), a Pearson Learning Solutions survey of nearly 2,000 U.S. teachers found that very few educators were using Twitter in class. Surprisingly, about half argued that social networks such as Facebook and Twitter are harmful to learning. Despite this research, Legaspi was undeterred. "A teacher for eight years, Legaspi said experience has taught him that a small group of students tend to dominate classroom discussions. During the seminar at Macworld, other teachers reported seeing broader student participation through Twitter" (Simon, 2011, para. 9). With numerous shy students in his class, Legaspi believed Twitter would give shy students a voice—one they might otherwise be frightened to share in front of a large group of students. Legaspi was right. Even his shiest student, who told CNN he had been bullied in the past, was emboldened by in-class Twitter chats, saying his tweets inspired his peers to see him "as an equal" (Simon, 2011, para. 15). Not only does Twitter give all students a voice in their classrooms, it gives them a voice around the world, which creates confidence and enhances independent learning. When students begin using Twitter, some as early as first grade, they learn to build a network of resources for learning. There's more on the power of a Personal Learning Network in Chapter 4.

FACEBOOK

I can't think of a better anecdote for using Facebook as a global learning tool than one about conducting research for this book. Because of my interest in global learning, I make a point of connecting with people from all over the world on Facebook. Of the thousands of friends I have, I would estimate that more than one third of them are connections from dozens of countries outside of the United States. While I have many anecdotes about global learning skills from my own experience as a classroom teacher, I wanted to know how other teachers are using social media to improve their craft and to connect their students with a global audience. What better way to learn how people use social media, I thought, than to talk to my own Facebook friends about it? So, I posted this question to my Facebook newsfeed: "How do you communicate with students and educators globally? What tools do you use?" Within minutes, teachers began sharing stories about communicating with other educators and students in faraway places like Saudi Arabia, Malaysia, Singapore, Korea, and Pakistan. They explained how they were collaborating with learners around the world with Skype, Google, Facebook, and Twitter. They were creating Facebook pages and groups, which facilitate conversations about best practices, common interests, books, cultures, and just about anything students and teachers wanted to discuss.

Sue Annan, who works at St. Brelade's College in the Jersey Channel Islands, was part of this Facebook conversation. She explained how she engages other English language teachers and learners, using Twitter and the #ELTChat Facebook group that she moderates. This Facebook group engages a remarkable worldwide collection of global learners, who unite in cyberspace with the goal of helping each other improve their practices. Annan explained it this way on my Facebook page: "We had to offer two different chat times 12 noon and 9 PM to maximize contact with every continent. I would

©Robert Churchill/Thinkstock Photos

say that between the twitter and Facebook sites, we are looking at 3–4,000 members, and almost every country is represented. For me, the contexts differ, as do the solutions on offer from teachers in differing situations. I learn new ways of doing things, with and without technology; I have a ready system of help when needed" (Annan, 2014). How can Facebook be used for education, I've been asked when presenting at schools and conferences. This example of reaching out to friends on a social network and igniting a conversation about best practices, along with participating in a group on Facebook where educators share stories, links to articles, and sample lessons, demonstrates how social media constructs an ongoing conversation about learning with stakeholders from countries all over the world.

INSTAGRAM

On a cool fall day, 12th graders at World Journalism Preparatory School in Flushing, New York, snap pictures and record video of the happenings at school. They annotate the pictures, putting captions on them that tell the stories beyond the image. It's always a news day in Starr Sackstein's journalism class. Students upload the graphics, videos, and captions to Instagram and share them to the class Twitter stream, using the hashtag #WJPSnews for their peers, their teacher, and the world to see. In addition to the newspaper, students who document the days at school, seniors in AP Literature and Composition take pictures and videos of classwork to allow for transparency; now parents can enjoy their children's learning and even join the conversation if they wish. By now, the impact Instagram has on global learning is likely clear, but Sackstein amplifies the point.

> Documenting our learning always has value. The transparency allows for students to share what they are learning in real time and for them to also have access to the moments that made learning, at a later time. By using the social media outlets, students can easily go back to what happened in class well after it is over. In addition

to being able to revisit learning, by making their learning visible to the world, they're able to elicit feedback from a variety of voices to enhance their experiences. (2014)

SOCIAL NETWORKING

Any feedback WJPS students receive on their Instagram streams or on the class Twitter hashtag builds on a conversation that originates in the classroom, carrying the discussion into cyberspace. The information students provide, coupled with the feedback and any questions they receive from people outside of their classroom via social media, makes them global teachers and learners. Sackstein reports that her own Personal Learning Network, including people who follow Sackstein's Instagram account and the #WJPSnews stream, contributes to these student-created online conversations. This kind of social networking in education is of paramount importance to the growth of these young adults as digital learners. They are accessing informative resources from around the world, using their teacher's PLN; this is a global learning skill that must be discussed and practiced often, so students will continue to use the skill even after they leave the class where they learned it.

Instagram student activity screenshot

● ● ● ● REFLECTION

Reflect on social media for inspiring global learners and interacting with resources from around the world. What are you doing in your own classroom or school to integrate social media into everyday teaching and learning? If you are still concerned about using Twitter, Facebook, or other social networks in class, consider constructing a pilot team of students, teachers, parents, and administrators to interact with one another and with people outside of your school, using one or two social networks. The pilot team can provide feedback about the experience and perhaps even produce a screencast video of its experiences using social media to become global learners. Once other education shareholders are using the same social networks, the screencast can be shared with everyone, highlighting the benefits of social learning.

CHAPTER
3

Digital Publishing

Storytelling is important. Part of human continuity.

—Robert Redford, actor

The boy I'll call Jose was quiet to the point of being labeled an introvert by several of my colleagues. In the traditional grades world, he was typically in the C-D-F range in most classes. On more than one occasion when I had asked students to write something in a notebook, Jose gazed into space or buried his head in his arms folded on his desk. He flatly refused to pick up a pencil—that is, if he had a pencil. Jose was a smart kid. The rare times he offered opinion to peers in small groups (he'd never comment on academic topics to me or to the entire class), his discourse was thoughtful and intelligent. When we worked on computers, if Jose was interested in the material, his star would shine; he loved the Internet. So, one day, I gave Jose a blog and told him and the rest of the class to write about any subject or area of interest in which they had expertise. He shrugged and stared at the ceiling. "What do you mean?" he asked in a whisper. I reiterated the unusually simple direction. "Write about anything!" So, he did. He also shared his content with the world and immediately became a global learner.

THE PERSONAL BLOG

Jose loved mobile applications and electronic devices. When students received personal blogs on a classroom Kidblog site, Jose wasted little time posting articles and reviews about mobile devices and his favorite apps. Google Glass was a relatively unknown device at the time, so Jose began researching this new product. Then, he posted an article explaining just what Glass was about, and he published it for his classmates and other blog enthusiasts to see. What happened next was remarkable. Jose, for the first time since he'd joined my class months earlier, had a voice. Within a couple of days, 80 comments were added to Jose's Google Glass blog post from inquiring young minds and even a few adults. Not only had Jose become an active member of a class he'd previously disdained, he broke down the walls and joined a universe of global learners. Many educators are realizing the power of blogs as digital publishing tools. "Benefits extend beyond the classroom. Introverted students tend to share more online than they do in person; blogging is an invaluable way for me to get to know them better as people and students. It's also great to see reserved students garnering attention from their peers" (Lampinen, 2013).

Blogs are surprisingly simple for teachers to set up for students. Sites like Kidblog, created by teachers for teachers, offer a free service and give educators the ability to build a learning management system. That is, you can manage a classroom website that contains all student blogs arranged in any way you like. A learning management system, LMS, increases user-friendliness by making it easy for teachers to locate all students' blog posts in one space. Similarly, students can quickly find their peers' blogs and comment on them, generating an interactive online conversation. Many teachers like the control that Kidblog provides, as it features moderation tools that make it difficult for students to post anything inappropriate, without the teacher seeing it. Teachers of older students may prefer Wordpress or Blogger, which give students more flexibility and freedom. These are fine tools but they increase the need for emphasis of appropriate use, which is always an important lesson.

STORYBIRD

Some elementary teachers believe that digital learning tools are only for teenagers. "My 8-year-olds can't post stories online," these skeptics sometimes suggest. When teachers see tools such as Storybird, they quickly become enthusiastic about the prospect of launching their students into cyberspace. A web-based content creation tool, Storybird isn't just for elementary students. Young writers gravitate to Storybird, though, because it

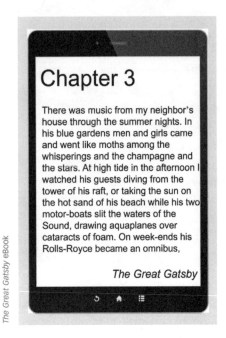

comes with a massive library of graphics that can easily be dropped into a storyboard, giving authors, artists, and poets a graphic canvas on which to build a visual story. Like many online publishing sites and applications, Storybird is also a social network. Not only are young authors able to share their art to other social networks, they can actively engage with anyone who views their work in Storybird's onsite community. This feature ignites an amazing conversation that includes, in many cases, constructive feedback from readers, which helps the author contemplate how to improve future works. Digital publishing tools unite learners in a student-centered, workshop environment. In fact, Storybird almost automatically builds an in-class and online collaborative, turning the teacher from sage on the stage to more of a guide on the side, which always inspires students to achieve more independently.

TRANSFORMING TEACHING AND LEARNING WITH YOUTUBE

Many years ago, I sat in front of six educators who were interviewing me for a teaching position. This was my first-ever conversation about becoming a classroom teacher. Nerves prevailed, and I stumbled along recklessly. Just when I thought my anguish was about to end, one panelist asked me if I had any questions for the interviewers. "Do you show students movies? I think there is a lot to be learned from video." Only seconds passed before I realized that this was an unpopular query. Eyebrows furrowed and the response was a short, "We don't encourage too much of it." Sadly, when I was finally hired by a school district in a suburb of Cleveland, I remembered how nauseous I felt during that first interview and, specifically, the bizarre reaction to my question about using movies as an instructional tool. Because of this unsavory experience, I rarely employed the strategy in my early teaching career and any video I did use was haphazardly selected and poorly delivered. Many years later, I discovered the true power of video instruction—thanks in large part to YouTube. Brief interactive lessons became commonplace in my classroom, and I eventually built my own online library of YouTube video lessons and placed them on the how-to video site for educators, LearnItIn5.com. Now, video instruction is being used in schools worldwide, helping teachers engage students in many subjects that they might be otherwise disinterested in. YouTube, one of the largest social networks, is an amazing platform for digital publishing, especially considering how much children and teenagers love media. According to The Neilsen Company (2013), teens consume 112 hours of video every month. When teachers provide learning opportunities on YouTube and allow students to publish their own videos there, they make use of this hunger for visual media rather than ignoring what their students want most. With education sites that integrate instructional videos cropping up regularly, YouTube is one of the most influential digital publishing platforms available to global teachers and learners. YouTube's share option empowers publishers—both teacher and student—with its embed and link features. Now, global learners can combine publishing tools. A student might write a blog post about the evolution of mobile devices and embed a YouTube video about advanced eReaders into the blog post. The publisher might then share the post to Twitter, Facebook, and Pinterest. In a matter of minutes, this student becomes a content curator, digital publisher, and global teacher and learner. When has education ever been able to do so much?

● ● ● ● REFLECTION

What approach should you take and which tools should you use to help your students become digital publishers? Meet with several colleagues, administrators, and parents and discuss the possibilities of building a library of content that represents your class and your school. What are the ramifications of allowing your students to publish online for the world to see? What barriers exist? Is there a need for universal publishing policy at your school and, if there is, what will this policy look like? Can you write a policy with fidelity that does not inhibit your students' ability to create and share content with a global audience?

CHAPTER
4

Building a Personal Learning Network

As a potential connected school leader, you now have to build a PLN. Click on and connect with us.

—Spike Cook, author of *Connected Leadership:*
It's Just a Click Away

S hawn Storm teaches social studies at a middle school in Quakertown, Pennsylvania. Storm is the epitome of a global learner. Sure, he is a teacher, but it takes a global learner to understand how to connect with resources around the world to enhance learning. When worldwide connections are made and these connections and resources are shared with students, all people involved become global teachers and learners. This is the power of social media in education, and Storm is a fine example of how 21st-century teachers are maximizing the immediacy and outreach of social networks, in order to influence students in our digital world. Storm's explanation of social media integration in his classroom illustrates how this approach helps students build a Personal Learning Network (PLN) while breaking the barriers of the traditional brick and mortar classroom.

> Twitter has revolutionized the way I approach teaching and more importantly learning. My students are now able to share their learning with anyone in the world and our classroom's walls no longer exist. Over the last three years, my students have had amazing opportunities to connect with other classrooms from Australia, Kenya, Canada, Bosnia, and almost every state in America. We have engaged in learning opportunities, including virtual debates, mystery Skypes, poetry summits, and guest speakers. My students tweet and post to our class Instagram accounts daily using our academic team's hashtag, #teamhonorsms, and to our district and school's hashtag as well. We post pictures of our daily learning, share our work with blogs, and look for experts about the topics we are learning (I just sent a message out this morning looking for a storyteller and within ten minutes made a connection with someone who tells stories in the mode of an African griot). (2014)

A GLOBAL LEARNING NETWORK

With an entire world of educators and resources at our fingertips, building a PLN can be a daunting task. Students who participate in social media tend to connect with friends and, in some cases, with family members. Few students comprehend the value of the PLN as an individual's most powerful source of learning. "The idea of a PLN is that it is a network of sources that help an individual personalize his or her learning" (Whitby & Anderson, 2014, p. 28). The idea of personal learning networks is still in its infancy. The online PLN started around 2007 but didn't become popular until about 2010 or even later. Now, many educators use Twitter,

Facebook, and LinkedIn to build Internet-based networks for professional development. They share links to education articles along with useful web tools, and they participate in live Twitter chats, using hashtags, which aggregate tweets into one stream. Teachers are using PLNs to become global learners. But what if we empower our students starting at a very young age with this same ability to build a worldwide network of teachers and resources? Is it feasible that a student PLN could create independent learners, while freeing up time for teachers to enhance learning through coaching and guidance rather than traditional teaching? Concordia University professor Bernard Bull (2013) makes a strong argument for the student PLN as a global learning tool.

A student personal learning network is, therefore, a rich and ever-growing series of connections with people, resources, and communities around the world . . . connections that allow us to grow in knowledge, skill, ability and perspective. What if we spent more time thinking about the networks that students are building as they go through their schooling years? What are the tools and technologies that they use and how are they using them? One of many connections in this network will likely be one or more teachers. It will also include classmates, family members, community members, and others with whom they learn and interact in the physical world. As it expands, it will also include people far beyond the walls of the home, school and community. What if we made the building of such a network a central part of the curriculum, inviting students to keep a log or journal of their growing network and how this network is empowering them to learn, how it is expanding their knowledge and perspective? How are they building a meaningful network? This would genuinely turn schools into places of fishing lessons. Students can interview people around the world, tutor and be tutored, take part in formal and informal learning communities, take part in Twitter chats and Hangouts, learn from and engage in the

(Continued)

(Continued)

blogosphere, experience the power of working on a meaningful project in a distributed/virtual team, participate in a massive open online course (or design and teach one), share resources through social bookmarking and other technologies, host and take part in webinars, and build new online and blended learning communities around topics of personal value, need, and interest. Over time, the students may not only build a personal learning network but also venture into starting their own personal teaching networks, being agents of change and positive influence in the digital world and beyond.

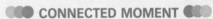

CONNECTED MOMENT

Many adults are just now connecting globally; they have small but growing personal learning networks that change often, according to their needs. Some educators have PLNs that have helped them improve professionally for years. If we teach children how to create amazing PLNs, beginning as early as elementary school, the possibilities for learning both in and out of the classroom are limitless.

WHERE TO FIND PLN MEMBERS

Global learners and teachers are in many surprising places—social networks, classrooms, digital publishing sites, blogs, forums and more. However, every friend, neighbor, peer, and social connection is not perfect for an individual's PLN. Author and education technology expert Steven Anderson amplifies this point in *The Relevant Educator*, explaining how to build a useful personal learning network: "I make changes all the time, adding new people to follow and unfollowing those that don't provide any value to my learning any more. Make it your own. It is personal, after all"

(2014, p. 29). Educators must teach their students this invaluable lesson. This is no small task, though, as most students will have no idea where to begin to locate useful PLN members. Following is a list of tips to share with students, who are creating a new, educational PLN.

4 WAYS FOR STUDENTS TO LOCATE VALUABLE PLN MEMBERS

1. Follow popular, young Twitter users and their followers: While they are few, there are Twitter users who are young and accomplished. Teen author/presenter, Adora Svitak (@adorasv), is one example. Svitak is a prodigy who advocates for feminism and progressive education and has over 5,000 Twitter followers. Svitak's Twitter network is filled with many young global learners, whom other students might be interested in adding to their own PLNs. Teach students to click the Twitter link of the followers of someone they admire, like Svitak. Twitter will populate a page with pictures and descriptions of these followers. View what these people are sharing and discuss what makes their content valuable.

2. Use Twitter's #Discover feature: Twitter's #Discover page is a powerful search engine, which allows users to browse popular accounts using a simple keyword search. This can be a fun activity that doubles as a research project. Teachers should model this search with students and show them how to separate the wheat from the chaff. For example, if I'm interested in architecture, I would type this term into the #Discover search field and review the accounts that the search returns. I'm likely to find something such as Architectural Digest (@ArchDigest). Instruct students to open account descriptions that interest them to see what content the person or company is sharing. What makes someone's tweets beneficial is an important question that students should learn to ask themselves and friends often, during this activity.

3. Explore other social networks: Although many connected educators associate their Personal Learning Networks with a group of people they follow on Twitter, it's important to note that the best PLNs are composed of people and resources across numerous social networks. Take time to explore other online communities that may contain quality members not found on Twitter. If you are an English teacher, or if your students read often, consider searching a site like Goodreads or Figment for PLN members. Goodreads is a social network for readers. People rate books, review books, create "to-read" libraries and interact with other readers. Students who love suspense might explore by genre and find peers who are reading the same books they read. Like Twitter or Facebook, Goodreads can be set up to send alerts through the mobile application or via e-mail, when PLN members recommend or review a book. Figment is a social network for writers. Like Storybird, writers can publish to Figment and create a network, filled with other authors. Imagine how writers will grow, when they interact with others in their peer group.

4. Find bloggers of interest: Chapter 3 covered blogging as a necessary digital publishing skill. When students become active bloggers who share their content with the world, they will likely become active blog readers, too. Bloggers tend to be experts on particular topics. Teach students how to use Internet search tools to locate experts in their areas of interest and in your subject area. Then, teach them how to subscribe to many blogs using an aggregator (Chapter 5 explains the magic of the content aggregator). Bloggers may turn out to be the most valuable members of your students' PLNs.

● ● ● ● REFLECTION

Do you have a PLN outside of friends and family members? Take a moment to consider the people in your network who provide the most value to your everyday learning. How did you find them? Can you pass on your experience with building a PLN to your students? What barriers exist in teaching students to create a powerful network of global teachers? Apart from the tips shared in this chapter for finding prized PLN members, consider other necessary lessons for students about constructing a digital network of teachers and learners. Do you have an effective Appropriate Use Policy (AUP)? If not, consider how crafting a PLN should fit into guidelines for Internet and social media use. If you do have an AUP, review it with other shareholders and decide if it needs to be updated to empower students to build Personal Learning Networks.

Using Aggregators to Create, Maintain, and Share Content

I'm happy to be content-maker as well as curator, so I'm happy to also be a presenter for amazing things.

—Jason Silva, filmmaker and philosopher

This book identifies five essential skills for global learning. While these are precise skills that involve particular tools, they are embedded in one underlying skill that is arguably the foundation of the digital world—content curation—a crucial part of learning that I've trumpeted in other places but because it's so important, I will emphasize it again here. "At the risk of exaggeration, let me begin this chapter by saying that understanding content curation may be the most important part of 21st-century education" (Barnes,

> Today, research is the beneficiary of content aggregators, which make research enticing and curation fun.

2014, p. 9). Curating content is the art of creating, maintaining, managing, and sharing written or visual information. I used to say that comprehending this concept isn't nearly as important as effectively completing it. However, as global learners evolve, I believe it's important for them to understand exactly what content curation is and how to become expert curators. Beginning as early as first grade, students are creating and sharing content. They don't always understand the ramifications of their actions, though, and when teachers say, "You will be judged by what you curate," which they should be saying, this can be confusing to students who are new to curation. The best way to help students understand how to become proficient curators and why they should be is to teach them the muscle behind aggregators.

SCOOP.IT

I used to hate teaching research. For 15 years, I broke down every step of the research process into tiny pieces, emphasizing citation styles and forcing students to write quotes on 3X5-inch index cards. We spent weeks looking up facts about the ancient civilizations, famous people, or other boring history topics in encyclopedias, old magazines, and even older nonfiction books. This process was agonizing and generally useless, unless you consider instilling a hatred of research in young people a valuable endeavor. The advent of the Internet ignited a new enthusiasm toward research, but it took several years before teachers started giving up old research strategies, including teaching every aspect of citing sources and jotting down quotes on note cards. Today, research is the beneficiary of content aggregators, which make research enticing and curation fun. Scoop.it, for example, organizes information from many sources into one place, essentially doing the work that index cards, outlines, and research papers used to do. With both a web platform and a mobile application, Scoop.it empowers users to do just what the name says, scoop information from anywhere, annotate it (no need for the old research paper), and share it with a global audience. In an article for *TeachThought* (2013), author and education technology expert Leanna Johnson explains the benefits of Scoop.it:

> Curation is a valuable skill for today's learner. In a culture of content overload, members that provide great content to their audience will be recognized leaders in network communities. Optimally, we equip students to differentiate good content from bad in preparation for their further education and careers. Curating an online topic (and allowing comments) also increases self-awareness and provides additional insight from others. The nuances of sharing content and writing to an audience become much better understood through interactivity between the curator and participating audience.

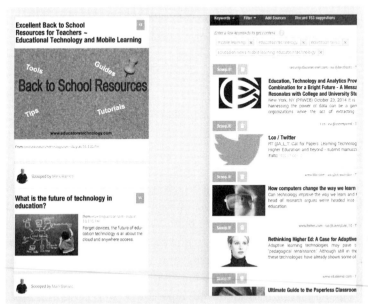

Johnson underscores the responsibility of teachers to help students—content curators—distinguish good and bad information, which has been an underlying theme throughout this book. As alluded to earlier, our students are already creating, maintaining, and sharing content. We must teach them how to do this in a way that will improve their digital footprint, while making them noteworthy global resources for learning. Scoop.it simplifies this lesson, as teachers can easily model locating useful stories, pictures, podcasts, and videos, using Scoop.it's intelligent search tool. Keyword searches on Scoop.it bring back a variety of content from sources such as Twitter, YouTube, news sites, and blogs. Periodic discussions after keyword searches about what is valuable and why students might decide to add something to their Scoop.it page will help them hone their curation skills.

 CONNECTED MOMENT

Chapter 4 examined building a Personal Learning Network as the go-to resource for global teaching and learning. While building an audience of worldwide connections is an integral piece of global learning, understanding how to effectively curate content from and for a PLN is equally important. The content we share composes our digital footprint, so we must curate content carefully.

FEEDLY

In Chapter 3, I emphasize the benefits of blogging as a digital publishing skill. It's certainly worth noting that when educators and interviewers ask me about the most important thing teachers can do to engage students, I say unequivocally that every student from the time they can write—maybe even sooner—should be publishing a blog and viewing other blogs. WordPress, the most popular blogging platform in the world, reports that writers publish more than 61 million blog posts every month, which are read by more than 400 million people worldwide. A possibly more important statistic is that 55 million new comments are posted to blogs monthly; a number that underscores the impact blogging has on the global learner. "Blogs continue to be highly popular around the world, and we're now seeing a trend that's potentially even bigger: publishers are using WordPress to create all kinds of sites beyond blogs—news sites, company sites, magazines, social networks, sports sites, and more" (WordPress, 2014). These statistics and information must not be underestimated. It's clear that digital publishing is becoming the primary method of sharing content worldwide. With billions of pages of content being created in multiple languages (over 3 million monthly posts in Spanish, another 1.5 million in Portuguese, and close to 1 million in French), distinguishing good content from bad is a monumental task requiring a keen understanding of precisely what makes content valuable.

Obviously, students can't read millions of web pages every month. This is where an aggregator like Feedly simplifies curation. Feedly is one of many available blog aggregators, and it's possible that teachers and students may find a different one that they prefer. In fact, using more than one content aggregator is not only acceptable, but in many cases it's preferable. I use Scoop.it and Feedly, because each tool offers something that the other doesn't. For example, Scoop.it has a subscription feature, allowing users to share the content they curate automatically with a large audience. Blog posts can be "scooped" and shared instantly with Scoop.it. Conversely, Feedly is mainly about collecting blog content and organizing it into categories for easy retrieval of desired information. Consider the clout of this tool for global learners. With Feedly, teachers and students can organize class blogs into specific groups, making access to particular content abundantly easy. Teachers might want students to collaborate on a research project, using their own personal blogs and then placing the individuals in each group into a specific Feedly category. So, if Jesse, Lilly, Emma, and Roberta are researching and writing about major role players in the Civil Rights movement, their blogs could be assigned to a Feedly category called Civil Rights. Other research groups might be placed in categories such as The Revolution, WWII, and Famous

Women. Students could create similar categories of their preference, giving them control of how they design their own digital libraries. Recall the WordPress statistics shared earlier in this section. Students might help each other identify informative content in various areas of interest and generate categories about that content and add the blogs they believe to be useful to those categories. Now, when bloggers from around the world publish valuable content, teachers and students can share that content with their PLNs, using Feedly's integrated social share feature. This is how experts curate content and if we teach students how to use the tools that will make them experts, learning improves exponentially.

HOOTSUITE

Global learners are always improving their curation methods and this involves exploring new content tools. Eventually, curators may use 10 or more web tools and social networks to create, maintain, and share information. HootSuite is one service that manages multiple sites in one place. While Scoop.it and Feedly empower users to gather information from multiple sources, HootSuite puts social networks and blogs in one place, so they can be administered together on one screen on your computer or mobile device. Imagine opening a page on your laptop, tablet, or smartphone and your Facebook, Twitter, LinkedIn, Google+, and WordPress blog all appear in perfect rows. Maybe you want to read your Facebook newsfeed, then send a tweet, then share your most recent blog post. In the old days (about 2008), you would have to navigate to these networks and work from within each individual platform. Reading, tweeting, and sharing content from five or six tools could take an hour or more. With an aggregator like HootSuite, a power content curator can read multiple posts in three or four streams and routinely share a variety of content across many networks with a few quick swipes or mouse clicks. HootSuite's flexibility puts screen options in the users' hands. If you're a Twitter power user, for example, you might want your main HootSuite screen to contain multiple Twitter features, such as "sent tweets," "messages," and "favorites." HootSuite and similar companies realize that curators have many needs, and they are constantly upgrading their services, in order to evolve along with the skills of global learners.

● ● ● ● REFLECTION

Some teachers are using aggregators to share student activities and conversations with their PLNs. How might teaching and learning change in your classroom, if you used this strategy? Are your students capable of using an aggregator? Brainstorm ideas for helping your students understand what aggregators do and how they can use them to improve their own content curation.

Conclusion

A courageous group of seventh graders took a chance one night a long time ago. I asked them to watch a political event on a streaming newsfeed, something that back then was relatively unknown. The 12-year-olds didn't have smartphones or tablet computers, on which to view the event, while playing with friends or babysitting younger siblings. Most would sit at a desk in a home office or bedroom and fumble their way to the online broadcast. The next step was equally foreign. I invited them to participate in an online chat using a standalone message board. The education websites that mimic Facebook and Twitter didn't exist, and using a social network wasn't an option (I wasn't sure what social media was back then). The students located the online broadcast and commented on the message board. I realized that this was a new way of learning, but I had no idea what was to come.

A year later, a new batch of students had their own private online platforms, each located in one website, which became a neatly organized learning management system (LMS). Students could write essays on their own web pages contained within our classroom website; they could upload slideshows and other presentations; they could maintain pictures, videos, and other graphics. Eventually, all lessons and models were placed in this online LMS, located at www.barnesclass.com.

> We hadn't yet given our classwork to the world, or maybe we had, and I simply didn't realize it, but when students began sharing projects online they were also breaking down the barriers of the classroom and becoming global learners.

Back then, I told colleagues and friends that teaching and learning was becoming web-based. Surprisingly, I had no idea what that statement really meant and how the classroom website would turn my students and me into global teachers and learners. What I originally thought was nothing more than a repository for activities, lessons, and projects morphed into a flat classroom, which is, in essence, a global classroom. While I wasn't attempting to be a global teacher or to create global learners, I realized that the classroom website, which contained its own blogging platform, a message board, public and private comment features, and a built-in email system created an online social network. Few, if any, of my students were on Facebook or Twitter; I had a dormant Twitter account back then and was under the impression that Facebook was a poor man's MySpace. Although I eventually learned the benefits of the leaders in social media for education, they weren't needed then because I had unwittingly built a social network of my own for my classroom.

We began discussing class activities and projects online, and students collaborating had their own group sites on our LMS. They would post research reports, discussions, and project activities in the private group and, eventually, share their work with the rest of the class and, best of all, with parents, administrators, and friends from other schools. We hadn't yet given our classwork to the world, or maybe we had, and I simply didn't realize it, but when students began sharing projects online, they were also breaking down the barriers of the classroom and becoming global learners. My students were revolutionizing teaching and learning, and I was joining them on an incredible, if somewhat frightening, journey.

With each passing year, new students came to my classroom. They brought with them skills and resources that their predecessors didn't possess. Smartphones, iPods, Kindles, and other electronic devices became staples of learning and were seamlessly integrated into our daily activities. We started using Twitter, YouTube, Kidblog, Goodreads, and other social networks, which were soon linked within our classroom website, which remained our online home base. Almost everything students discussed or created was shared with a global audience. The possibilities for learning were boundless.

UNIVERSAL TEACHING AND LEARNING

Shelly Terrell, a wonderful educator whom I first encountered on Twitter years ago and then met in person at a major education event, invited me to help her and a few others organize an online global learning conference, called the Reform Symposium. At the time, I had no idea what was involved in organizing a major education conference. I had attended many in-person conferences, but I wasn't sure what an online conference looked like. A few months later, thousands of people from more than 100 countries attended RSCON (Reform Symposium Conference). For three days, they gathered in web-based presentation rooms, viewing online presentations from dozens of speakers from around the world. Although I had been communicating with people as far away as Australia for years on Twitter, this online education conference represented the first time I really considered myself a global learner. It was an epiphany that changed my life.

After the Reform Symposium, I began writing more about online learning and the influence that social media has on education. As mentioned in the previous section, mobile devices and social networks became commonplace in my classroom, but we still didn't fully comprehend their power. My students blogged daily and commented on work written by classmates, peers in other classes, and even on the work of others from around the world. This was long before the launch of the Corwin Connected Educators Series, and even if I didn't realize it at the time, the global teachers and learners I was encountering every day in my classroom and in cyberspace were paving the road to this book.

You may work in a school that is short on computers and is chained to policies that forbid the use of electronic devices and social media in the classroom. The lack of technology and archaic policies should not deter you from global learning. Regardless of how ill equipped some schools may be for 21st-century education, our students are ready to embrace modern technology; most arrive prepared to engage with teachers and resources online. You have global learners in your classroom and they have a universe of resources at their fingertips. And now you have no less than five skills to teach them. Our children are global learners, and they need global educators to teach them how to navigate the digital world. I can't think of a more honorable calling.

References

Barnes, M. (2013). *The 5-minute teacher: How do I maximize time for learning in my classroom?* Alexandria, VA: ASCD.

Barnes, M. (2013). *Role reversal: Achieving uncommonly excellent results in the student-centered classroom.* Alexandria, VA: ASCD.

Barnes, M. (2014). *Teaching the iStudent: A quick guide to using mobile devices and social media in the K–12 classroom.* Thousand Oaks: Corwin.

Barnes, M. (2015). *Assessment 3.0: Throw out your grade book and inspire learning.* Thousands Oaks, CA: Corwin.

Bull, B. (2013, November 13). Helping students develop personal learning networks [Web-log message]. Retrieved from http://etale.org/main/2013/11/22/helping-students-develop-personal-learning-networks/

Cook, S. (2014). *Connected leadership: It's just a click away.* Thousand Oaks, CA: Corwin.

Covili, J. (2012). *Going Google: Powerful tools for 21st-century learning.* Thousand Oaks, CA: Corwin.

Curry, B. (2014). *All hands on deck: Tools for connecting educators, parents, and communities.* Thousand Oaks, CA: Corwin.

Johnson, L. (2013, February 18). Why Scoopit is becoming an indispensable learning tool [Web-log message]. Retrieved from http://www.teachthought.com/technology/why-scoopit-is-becoming-an-indispensable-learning-tool/

Lampinen, M. (2013, April 8). *Blogging in the 21st-century classroom.* Retrieved from http://www.edutopia.org/blog/blogging-in-21st-century-classroom-michelle-lampinen

A live look at activity across Wordpress.com. (2014). Retrieved from http://en.wordpress.com/stats/

Madden, M., Linehart, A., Cortesi, S., Gasser, U., Dugger, M., Smith, A., & Beaton, M. (2013, May 21). *Teens, social media, and privacy.* Retrieved from http://www.pewinternet.org/2013/05/21/teens-social-media-and-privacy/

Mystery Skype: Connecting classrooms around the world. (2014, February 1). [Web]. Retrieved from https://www.youtube.com/watch?v=GZdMnkWHG7s#t=27

Nielsen, L. (2014, October 26). Digital footprint: Advice from the experts at tech forum NY [Web-log message]. Retrieved from http://theinnova tiveeducator.blogspot.com/2014/10/digital-footprint-advice-from-experts.html

The Nielsen Company. (2013). *The Teen Transition: Adolescents of Today, Adults of Tomorrow.* New York, NY: The Neilsen Company. Retrieved from http://www.nielsen.com/us/en/insights/news/2013/the-teen-transition–adolescents-of-today–adults-of-tomorrow.html

Simon, D. (2011, June 09). *Twitter finds a place in the classroom.* Retrieved from http://www.cnn.com/2011/TECH/social.media/06/08/twitter .school/index.html?hpt=us_1

Sinanis, T., & Sanfelippo, J. (2014). *The power of branding: Telling your school's story.* Thousand Oaks, CA: Corwin.

Whitby, T., & Anderson, S. (2014). *The relevant educator: How connectedness empowers learning.* Thousand Oaks, CA: Corwin.